Fighting

The

Dragon

Fighting The Dragon

by

Diana Kay Lubarsky

Cover Design by
Sarah Rikaz
www.SarahRikazCreative.com

TOLIFE...Ink

Buffalo N.Y.

Write The Book You Want To Read

Breezes was previously published in RAIN Magazine 2017.
Birth (now called Talia's Birth), Morning Star (now called Special Girl),
I Love You and My Father's Store were previously published in
Seeds of...Volume II: An Anthology of Pacific Northwest Writers.
Edited by Mary Jane Nordgren
A TAWK Press Publication, copyright © 2015

Printed in the United States of America

ISBN: 978-0-578-20281-5
The main category of the book —Poetry —
First Edition

TOLIFE...Ink
Buffalo NY
Write The Book You Want To Read

Thank you D.K. for this wonderful book. The richness of the writing is deceiving with words that are familiar and soothing. Yet with each reading, more complex meanings begin to jump off the pages of this book. The stories are real, heartfelt and very personal while still sounding a resonate chord in each one of us that is as true to us as it is the writer ... Susan Schmidlin

Co-owner of the Schmidlin Angus Farm, as well as an avid blogger of humorous farm stories. Her work has been published in RAIN Magazine and several other publications.

Diana's poems are not to be gobbled up like popcorn, but savored, so the soul can absorb the wisdom that rolls onward like waves at the ocean. My heart forces me to read them again & again. ... Shannon Brown

A retired teacher who loves writing enough to have started a school newspaper. She is published in many educational materials, such as the nationally certified GLAD program.

A good poet pays attention and gives voice to the truths of human condition. Diana's writing speaks to and of our truths, whether the topic is parenthood, loss, aging or birth. She calls it as she sees it, sometimes with humor, sometimes not, but always spot on and true. ... Ann Farley

A writer and poet whose work has appeared in several on-line sites and magazines including Voice Catcher, RAIN, and Verseweavers.

Diana Kay Lubarsky sees deep within a person. That insight, compassion and humor glow forth as she fights her dragon...and ours. ... M.J. Nordgren

A retired family physician, the author of "Early: Logging Tales to Human to be Fiction" and 7 other books.

Dedication

Every Monday morning a group of writers meet at the Senior Center in Forest Grove, Oregon. They call themselves Writers in the Grove. Collectively, these are the most talented, encouraging and uplifting people I have ever known. Individually, they are diverse and hysterically funny. This magnificent crew is led by Mary Jane Nordgren, an exceptional woman who, like all the others, has blessed me with her friendship. It is with a profound sense of gratitude that I dedicate this book to M.J. Nordgren and Writers in the Grove, for without these amazing people it would certainly never have seen the light of day.

Preface

Dragons come in all sizes, shapes and colors. Some people say they are invisible. Mine certainly aren't. They crop up and demand my attention at the most inopportune of times, frequently casting their shadow on the sunniest of days. I live with a wide assortment of Dragons, in one form or another. They are shape-shifters disguised as anger, guilt, sadness, disappointment, loneliness, anxiety or fear. And when they appear, raging battles suddenly consume my thoughts.

Whatever form your Dragon comes in, I hope it helps to know there are others out there fighting Dragons just as you are.

Keep fighting! We may not win every battle, but I truly believe we can win most of them... All while trying to make sense of this crazy world we live in.

POEMS

Breezes..........................12

God's Voice.....................14

Oregon Time....................15

Redwood Forest................16

Sand.............................17

Morning.........................18

Places I Hid....................20

Afraid...........................21

Shhh!...........................22

My Father's Store..............23

Walk Away......................24

Fishing..........................25

Surreal Woman.................26

Rose............................27

The Annual Visit...............30

Ari..............................31

Chocolates for Lilah...........32

Talia's Birth....................33

Multi-Tasking...................34

Luncheon Date............................36

Gift..37

Cancer......................................40

Special Girl...............................41

Thursday Afternoon Tea...............42

Diagnosis..................................45

The Waters Edge.......................47

Fighting The Dragon...................48

Mourning...................................50

Rosh HaShanah..........................54

Poverty, Charity, Giving

and Safety.................................55

The Mirror Has Two Faces............57

The New House..........................59

Ghosts......................................61

Time and Senses........................62

Stuck,.......................................63

New Writing Tablet......................64

National Holocaust

Remembrance Day......................65

The Sculptor..............................66

First Love....................................68

I Love You...................................69

Light..70

In-Between..................................72

Prayer......................................74

Today

BREEZES

The sun rides a clear course at dawn
Early breezes tumble through my hair
Greeting a world of quiet expectation
Choreographed by the wind

My days are ever changing
The footing uncertain
Alone in the morning light
I struggle to learn new dance steps
Each time the currents shift

Children, long since swept away by other breezes
Scattered by other winds
Plant and sow their seeds elsewhere

Through mid-day bluster
Elder wisdom quietly whispers
Celebrate this day
Do not waste time on what is gone
It is not an easy task

I breathe the afternoon hours one at a time
Each moment following the next
While the wind chimes spin
70 years, the dance remains forever new

Though allegiances tether me closer to home
The setting sun still wanes glorious when the day withdraws
And the cool wind, whether in my face or at my back,
Still breathes life into my soul

Like a worn cloth too often scrubbed, I know I am vanishing
The vibrant colors of youth seeping inward
Cradled by the breeze
And the song of the wind

I dance slower on these days of long hours
With others also faded from life's sun
We laugh about our journey
And hold hands
As we surrender our life's colors back to the earth
And ride the night wind home

Tomorrow I will pluck some weeds
And change the sheets
I will listen to music
And write a poem
I will call my friends, hug my love
And learn one more dance step before I sleep

God's Voice

I heard the voice of God today
As winter rustled through feathers
It was an awesome sound
Arriving with Canadian geese in spearhead formation
Directly overhead

Thousands of times I have glanced on high
And watched them stroke the wind
Rowing ever forward
As if heaving to some unheralded drummer
But never before did they pass directly overhead
And oh so close I thought I might stretch out my hand
To skim their soft white bellies as they swept passed

It was not until that moment I knew such a sound existed
The dancing of wind through feathered wings
An awesome sound, directly overhead for barely a second
Then swiftly rippling away

And all I could think
Was how very beautiful a sound it was
Surely this must be the sound of God's voice
Humming on a winter's afternoon
And certainly I will never be the same after having heard it

Oregon Time

My day is night in Afghanistan
My son sleeps while I breakfast
Tossing yesterday's crumbs to morning doves
Splashing in backyard puddles

My mind then reaches for a daughter
Nestled in the drought-stricken arms of the Gobi Desert
Fatigued after an afternoon in 110 degree sun
She clings to the single bottle of tepid water that is her lifeline
While I dance slowly with Oregon birds in the rain

My son joined the military
My daughter is a globetrotter
On her way to Mongolia as we speak

I look at their photographs on Facebook
Close my eyes to my small dreary existence
And try to imagine another life

Redwood Forest

A thousand altars stand
Ancient, burnished wood gleaming in sunlit slices
Guarding the path

I tread gingerly
Beneath the weight of a millennium

Dwarf within a sea of green
My eyes, beckoned by heaven's dappled sky
Rise toward the canopy of leaves, fringed and plaited
Where time and pulse all but cease

I stop
Rooted in ancient black soil
Holding gaze and breath
And feel a thousand forest eyes turn downward
Winking at me through fern, limb and wind

Acknowledging in floral whispers
The communion of our spirits
Though theirs be eternal and mine fleeting

Sand

My days are filled with sand
    Loose
    Swirling sand
    Some days choking me
    Other days warm and squishy beneath my feet

Some days the sand turns to ash
    Cascading down as tree embers
    Coating my car
    And the robin's nest

Other days the sand flows like tears
    Falling
        Falling
            Falling without end from a cloudless sky
    Into the hungry mouths of sewers and canyons
    Filling parched basins of subterranean aquifers

Then the sand returns
    Spinning my world
    A whirling dervish
    And a decade passes
    And I wonder who I am

I place both hand and foot print in the sand
And watch it fossilize
    Memories imprinted with my life
    Left for future generations if they care to look

Morning

I awaken to light
Eyes landing on pale yellow walls
Reminding me of buttercups smiling in the field
White tulle curtains seem to laugh
As they dance by the open window
And I know I am home

Ears awaken to the sound of his breathing
And down the block children at play
In the distance, lawn mowers and diesel trucks

And I know I have been safely delivered into tomorrow
And by the grace of God offered the chance to start again

Yesterday

Places I Hid

Behind the green club chair
Under the bathroom sink
Flattened against the wall beneath the bed

Not daydreaming
Hiding
Looking for a window of silence
Eating a forbidden apple
Frightened that I might be discovered

When I was older I sought green spaces
Long walks in dense woodlands
Gentle lights from heaven guiding my way
Not afraid until the house came into view
And I was visible again

Tiny, thin, frail little girl
The dreams were always the same
Transforming into a giant muscle-bound man
Who would beat everyone up
Then laugh

Afraid

Mornings were terrifying, as were daytimes and evenings
But mornings were the worst
The young girl knew the danger signals well
Imprinted from her earliest memories
Her day always written in her mother's black penciled eyebrows

The sound of mother's steps coming down the hall came first
Most days she heard the floor creak and could prepare
Other times mother just seemed to appear
As if from some malevolent vapor
That was the scariest

But the eyebrows would always reflect mother's mood
How harsh the day would become
And how far the child's soul would withdraw

Every now and then mother's eyebrows would relax
And the young girl dared scan the rest of mother's face
    for other clues

Alone times were always safest

Shhh!

Shush! Don't tell anyone
Tiptoe into that dark place near sleep
That distant empty space
Where unseen tears
Dampen your pillow
Shhh! Be silent
Not even a whisper
They wouldn't believe you anyhow

Diana Kay Lubarsky

My Father's Store

Brooklyn 1957

Wind and snow dance on concrete streets
Slicing through city canyons of pre-war brick
Tattooed with casement windows and iron laced fire escapes
This day, like all the others, shortened by winter's darkness

My father's hardware store smells like the kerosene
He keeps in the back room
I cut kitchen shades to measure with confidence born of youth
And likewise keys proportioned to locks

I am too young to carry 12 foot rolls of linoleum
The way father does, on his back, up six flights of stairs
But I help out each Saturday in the weeks before Christmas
Selling white china cups and bright red Christmas tree stands

The smell of kerosene, and the taste of piping hot bagels
Still brings me back to those days
Munching hot bagels on the ride home
In the days before the anger

Walk Away

The door slams
A familiar thud
I walk away to clear my head
Flee from wounding words
Pursuing solitude

Existence measured by foot falls and heart beats
"Remember to breathe," I tell myself
In, out, in again
Rhythm, to blot out pain
Long strides, to cleanse life's abrasions

A mile…Sometimes more
My body begins to sync with the earth's pulse
Connecting to a universal energy I cannot name
"Be calm," it whispers
As light slowly filters through my soul

I feel the shift
Rediscovering my center
Who and what I am
Acknowledging the inventory of broken promises and
    expectations
Theirs and mine

With each step my heart softens
As I balance life's checkbook
Weighing the price of love, and the price of darkness
But the wind has already changed direction
Spun me around
Pressing at my back as I turn and walk toward home

Fishing

I went fishing once
On a honeymoon with my first husband
We caught seven fish between us
And gave them away to the man who took our
    triumphant photograph

Two years later I gave away my first husband
And posed for the triumphant photograph by myself

Surreal Woman

Joined together with a surreal woman
That crazy lady locked within my soul
Deliverer of extremes
Creator of survival, brilliance, and anxiety disorders
Genetically inherited from a lunatic mom
And five thousand years of history
The two of us live beneath my skin
Bound in silence
Afraid to separate

Rose

(for Grandma Rose 1887-1962)

Night sheds its woolen sleeve
In grey twilight the rose appears
Petals pale and pink unfold toward my hand

The wooden table washed clean
Hides my initials, carved decades past on its underbelly
Our secret, though I suspect the rose knows

Clocks chime
Light strikes papered walls
Ivy trellises on yellow trees

Pablum spots, long swept away
Still dot the floor in the childhood kitchen of my mind
But grandmother's rose still smells as sweet
And I still bask in the light of her eternal love

Children

The Annual Visit

She breathed life into my reality
Shattering the silent wall of my existence with her song
Rising at dawn, fresh coffee brewing
Out for an early run before the sun fully awoke

"Good Morning Mamma" she sang as I opened my eyes
A smile lighting her lovely face
The scent of her awakening within me
    feelings long sequestered
An early embrace to start the day,
    with cream and sugar and a side of endless love

Floors buried beneath piles of clothes, books, bags,
    make-up, toothpaste, shoes
    wires, computers and iPads everywhere
Strange foodstuffs coming and going in Styrofoam boxes
Counter tops sticky with breadcrumbs, marmalade,
    coffee granules, a half-eaten plum
Clothes and wet towels draped on chairs, wooden doors,
    shower curtains

Then in a whisper, she is gone
The household restored to its quiet pristine order
I am so thankful that this blessed child returns home
    each year
To replenish her soul, and mine
To feel the cyclone of her life billowing through my world
As with a longing heart, I quietly await her return

Ari

Blue eyes peeping out from beneath a Star Wars blanket…
A 9 year-old blond Jedi
Scanning the room for invincible foes

His mind adrift in galaxies my old eyes no longer see
Until tired of extra-terrestrial battles
He returns to my arms and whispers
"I love you, grandma"

I smile and whisper into his precious face
"I love you too, Ari"

Chocolates for Lilah

Pretty boxes
Lined in a row
Pink and ribboned
With lilacs and perfume
Each filled with a chocolate
Bright colored treats
For my baby granddaughter, Lilah

Who plays in my yard
Plays in my heart
Fills me with promise
Tickles my soul
A rainbow of colors
I give back to this child
A rainbow of chocolate
Each in its place
A rainbow of colors for Lilah

Talia's Birth

Morning air shivers with the smell of birth
Blood, tears, joy, anticipation
My eyes hug the orb of mother and child
I lean closer, to watch the rise and fall of Talia's chest…
    half a hand-width in size

I inhale her exhale, weighing her life force
One day
And she has already surpassed her greatest challenge
She has survived
Life, love, endless possibilities await
Her little body smells of hope
Talia's eyes open and the world brightens

Multi-tasking

She races the clock with adrenalin pumped efficiency
Tumbling laundry from washer to dryer

Timing the oven baked casserole against
Computer emails awaiting response

Juggling chores like oranges
Trying to see how many she can keep up in the air
    at the same time

The Queen of multitasking
Until the school nurse calls and she races out of the house

Letting the day's tasks fall helter-skelter
No longer caring where they land

Detour

She lands at our door
Surrounded by children

A gale force wind of smiley faces
Leaving my hair blown and my heart aflutter
They whisk past
Grabbing the hamster and a diet coke

A runaway train speeding by
Fast tracking
Kids in tow

No time for hugs on this stop mamma
Check next week's schedule for further information

We are a last minute detour between doctor visits and pizza

Luncheon Date

Trying to know the stranger who was once my child
Sweet girl
Beautiful woman
Sitting across the table

Perfect features set in stone
Gradually becoming translucent to a mother's eyes
I see the scars life has inflicted on this cherished one

Wanting desperately to help, to ease her pain
Both of us knowing there is nothing I can do, but to love her

I stammer
The words never come out right when we are together
Always returning to "I love you"
Hoping it says enough
Knowing it doesn't

She scrutinizes my face when I say we need to talk
And I watch her brace, as if for a strike
It kills me
To have such an effect

Can't she tell? Doesn't she know yet?
All I want is for her to be happy
And when she tells me she cannot
I die inside

Gifts

Shadowy days lumber by
Alone in my thoughts
Memories whisper to my soul

Gifts, once sought, now inconsequential clutter
Boxes ribboned in glorious profusion remain intact
Pearls unstrung in velvet lined caskets

Today's most precious gift is a hug
The warmth of love
Perfumed color of family

In this day of time and travel
The only gift I seek is you
Returned home

Our family, once inseparable
Now forever divergent
Renders all other gifts meaningless

Illness

Cancer

Fold into my arms
And let me caress you with gentle strokes
My heart whispers between beats
I am here
I will not let go
Ever

Slowly we inhale
Ignore the pain
For this moment we are safe
Together
Friends
Having touched on a sunny afternoon
A moment that cannot be undone by death

Time rolls out before us
Days and nights
Inconsistent as snow flakes
And I wonder if we dare make a pact
That whoever arrives at God's table first
Saves a place for the other

Special Girl

Sweet child of mine with your funny little gait
Head down in forward thrust
Arms flapping at odd angles behind

Sweet child of my child
Running forward, sideways, zig-zag down the street
So fast I cannot catch you
Laughing

Sweet child of life
Each time you triumph
My heart celebrates
Each time you stumble
My heart cries

Have you noticed yet that you are a bit different
    than other children?
I think not
I hope you never do

Thursday Afternoon Tea

Quivering hands stretch, palm down
Searching the empty space
He has Prostate cancer
        Diabetes
        Dementia
        Ankylosing spondylitis

Years of life worn thin as rose petals
Skin as thin as rose petals
She reaches into the night air
Clasps his fingers
Still clinging to his smell and the comfort of his arms
Though he no longer remembers who she is

Long nights
Days etched in granite, as
Light lumbers slowly, traversing the sky
She waits
        As he climbs the stairs
        Rises from the toilet
        Puts on his shoes
        Grabs for her arm when his world spins

She waits
        Helps
        Pulls
        Pushes
        Catches
        Prods
        Screams to the wind!

Longing for Thursday afternoon
Respite…
Tea with women friends
Respite…
Her tether to the outer world

They meet
Aged and wrinkled with bright pink lipstick
Talk about husbands
Parkinson's
Heart failure
Hip fractures
Wheelchairs

She tells them she has a pebble in her shoe
And reaches for a tissue
Then returns home

In the evening her mind counts
Eleven women friends whose husbands died this year
Succumbed to
Age
Stroke
Ulcerative colitis
Pneumonia

She waits her turn
Wondering what Greece will look like in the spring
How sweet the apples will taste in fall
Trying to recall an ocean voyage
Salt water
Youth

A cry
She wakens uncertain if it was from her lips, or his
Checks to see if he is still breathing
Rolls him over to the left
His arm drapes across her shoulder
    Thin
    Frail
    Tremulous
    Yet familiar
I am here, she whispers
Wondering how much longer they will share this bed
Listening again to the sounds of his breath
Her mind searching for something else

Diagnosis

I   Breathe
Again
Once more
The doctor said I would live.....
Right after he pronounced the brain disease
     that crafted my symptoms

Oh God, how am I supposed to go on?
It is 3:00 am
I have become best friends with Internet Explorer
Tossing unfathomable questions into the void
Receiving instantaneous replies confirming my diagnosis

II The diagnosis hits again
A sledgehammer in the night striking my chest
Leaving me without breath

Long unrecognized warning signs
Dance before my eyes
Their message now clear
Tomorrow's dreams gone

III Some days, when there is no hope,
I walk on anyway
One foot in front of the other
I buy organic vegetables and premium fruits
I clean my clothes, make my bed, and visit the dentist
And I wonder, why? If there is no hope

I live in the shadow of death
Inexplicably drawn to darkness while
    searching for light
Avoiding the glare of day while mourning its loss
Seeking meaning even while rejecting it
Sadness, my comfort blanket, wrapped around
    my shoulders

IV In darkness, stalking the dawn
That tiny spark within
That is usually obscured by life's uproar
Refuses acknowledgement of inevitable loss
And forges ahead, leading me toward survival

The Water's Edge

Ocean waves crashing,
Exhaling seismic gusts of salt air in my face
Laughing tsunami, demanding my full attention
Drawing me out into the breathless soul of the universe
Allowing me to forget this morning's spoken words

Another crescendo, avalanche of water
Poseidon's arms stretch across the ocean
Reaching out to greet me

I step forward
Frothy fingers grab my ankles, then my knees
Pulling me into his embrace
My heart stands still

Do I go forward to dance with the gods
    in this universe of unfathomable depth?
Or walk back to engage the painful words
    now etched in this day's sand

Somberly weighing options at the water's edge

<u>Fighting The Dragon</u>

I know I am losing this battle...
His fiery breath is searing my face
His sharp scales are digging into my skin
His tail has begun winding around my ankles
The end is drawing near

Wait...
Haven't we done all this before?

You pop up out of nowhere
    and suddenly demand my full attention
Do you even have an appointment?
I don't think so!

Fighting a Dragon is exhausting
It drains all my energy

And do I really have time for your crap right now?
Other people depend on me, you know
Double-checking my calendar...
There are still a number of calls I need to make
Projects to finish
Reports to write
Bills to pay

Hell Dragon, stop drumming your claws!
I know there's a chance you will win someday
But not today!
Or for the foreseeable future

Go Away!
Bite someone else, if you must…

THIS DAY IS STILL MINE
And I will no longer waste my precious time
Playing your games

Mourning

I cannot mourn in front of my children,
I cannot share the sorrows and tears of age and illness
Nor cry from the depth of my heart
Nor speak of the profound and lingering losses
I cannot tell them of the pain I feel at times
They do not want to know

I cannot mourn with my children
They choose not to see the shriveled arms and shuffling gait
"You are fine,"
    They sing in their frantic dance of life
"You underestimate yourself,"
    They call over their shoulders
    As they race through sunny fields,
    Flying off to catch their young
    Leaving me far behind in their wake

Confident full-fledged adults,
With steam engine powered muscles
Their throttles smashed forward against infinity
They recognize on some transient level, I suppose
That I am something else
A specter of the mother they once had
Tho' purposely not examined too closely
For then they might have to acknowledge
    the proximity of loss
In their world of distant horizons

So I cannot mourn my losses with my children
But I thank God for my friends
Equal in age and weariness
We sit around the table
    stacking our wounds like poker chips
Unashamed confessions
Tethered with nods and sighs, handclasps and hugs

Learning from one another how to step forward
How to keep laughing
In spite of it all
To appreciate simple pleasures
And each other

We grieve and giggle on the same breath
Then breathe, grieve and giggle once again

And at day's end
I come away stronger for their strength
So that I can return to the children I adore and listen
    as they say
"See, I told you that you were okay"
Never comprehending how close to the edge
I was when first awakening to morning's light

But perhaps I am better off being able to glean from
    their perspective
Knowing that for now, this very moment
I truly am okay

Musings

Rosh HaShanah

Moments pass
Decades seem to rise and fall with each tide
I scan the horizon to see if I can find my reflection
    In forest and wind, earth and air, ocean and plain
What have I added to this world?
What have I received?

Counting Blessings too many to enumerate
    Yet so often invisible
This is a time of reflection
A stop sign in the road of hustle and bustle
    And mere survival of life

To all I have injured by plan, ignorance or indifference
    I ask your forgiveness
    And wish you Blessings for the New Year
To all who have sweetened my daily walk
    I thank you
    And wish you Blessings for the New Year

As leaves of red and gold sweep through the air
    Pressing the clock ever forward
I pray this New Year will also sweep
Health, goodness and compassion
    Into this world
    Into our homes
    And into all our lives

Poverty, Charity, Giving and Safety

A hundred envelopes a week arrive in my mailbox
Pleading their causes:
Support our firm, business, school, charity, foundation

Television commercials, squeezed between inane
    blocks of diversion
Beg for my dollars, quarters, pennies
With the wide frightened eyes
Of babies, puppies, wildlife,
    eroding glaciers and coral reefs

Neighborhood kids ring my doorbell
Would I support their football team, school trip, supply lists?
As they try to sell me cookies, wrapping paper
    and raffle tickets

And then there are the news reports
And political commentaries
Thousands of people in endless quests
On the verge of perishing
Bloody, thirsty, thin as vapor

Caught in the throes of hurricane, fire, flood
Or the wide jaws of conflict
Can I PLEASE send relief, NOW!

Each week I try
To send, give, mail, answer, at least one or two
But how to choose?

Some days when the human scream is just too loud
The pain too endless to bear
I close my purse, climb into bed
Pull the blanket over my head
And go to sleep

The Mirror Has Two Faces

Mirror, who are you today?
Who shall is see reflected in your face?
Rushed morning. I fly by. Quick glance in your silvery surface
Are all the hairs on my head swept in approximately
    the same direction?

The clock says there is still time
Back to the mirror for a closer look
Apply makeup
Nearer and further from your face I vacillate
    and assess
First the wrinkle comes into focus
Then the stray grey hair in my brow
    and the bump on my cheek
The longer I stare, the more imperfections I find

Perhaps a longer view would help my image
I walk in front of the floor length mirror
    and re-assess for a third time
Do the shoes match the outfit?
Which protrudes further my boobs or my belly?
Suck it in
Dear mirror, do I look into your face
    only to see my imperfections?

Silently my husband comes to my side
We stand shoulder to shoulder
    and gaze into the same mirror
A smile lights his face as he stares at my reflection
He says "You look so beautiful today"

I sigh, and melt into his arms
Reminding myself that the reflection I see in his eyes
    is all I need to go forth into this new day

He will be my mirror

The New House

I believe in ribbons of souls passing through the universe
Brushing against skin, sweet kisses of life
brightening daily paths

I believe in fate and spirits
And intergenerational memories of the land
    and its dwellings
And I am left to wonder why this new house
    doesn't speak to us

What sunlight drenched this place before we came?
What darkness filled its corners?
Upon our arrival she was torn down to a slab
A first step toward reconstructive elegance
Did she feel pain? Betrayal? Fear?
Did we remember to ask permission?

And when we built her up again to a new image
It was not her image
Not her song
She was re-built to our tune,
    our obdurate mid-life thrumming
An odd melody
Did she mind?

There never was a courtship…Nor love affair
Through all the tears and tatters and reconstructs
    we remained coldly detached
Professionals
Pride in our pieces, yet unable to feel the house tremble

We tumbled into her space
A quickly arranged marriage
Impromptu ceremony
Like a young virgin bride she was given away
Without consent of the spirits who lived in this space
None of us quite leaving our longing for the past behind

We have now lived within her walls for a year
In a marriage of convenience
But have yet to bless this house with a name
Perhaps that is why she does not speak to us

Ghosts

Twenty feet from the top
I turned and walked away
My mind seeing images
These eyes would not behold

Familiar ghosts snag my ankles
Impeding ascending trails
I crumble to the ground
And commune with tender earth instead

The pulse of life through decades flows
And windows frost and vision dims
I wonder if my ghosts, now friends
Will ever depart that I might see the mountain's crest

Time and Senses

The brown velour blanket stroked my face as I turned
Darkness, thick, rich and warm
Pulling me back into some nighttime void
Where dreams of nonsense make sense
Feet can stretch to infinity
And toes can wiggle
    without carrying the burden of my weight

My left arm emerges into morning cold
Long enough to slap the radio alarm
Silencing those strangulated voices
    and aberrational rhythms
    poking at my ears and dragging me into semi-consciousness
I yawn, tasting last night's coffee,
    and manage to open my eyes

Hushed only minutes earlier
    worldly sounds now make themselves heard
A train whistle
The roar of a truck
The ticking of my clock
My eyes focus on its iridescent white arms
    swimming on a circular black sea

It is 3:00 am
Time to get up and take my step-son to the airport

Stuck

Stuck
      Foot in the sand
      Life on hold
            Waiting for him to be ready
            Waiting for the bread to rise
            Waiting for the other shoe to drop
            Waiting for Godot

Afraid anything I start will be stopped
      By time, responsibility, obligation
      By someone else's need

Waiting for night
      When my fatigue can evaporate into the diversion
            Of books, television, puzzles, sleep

Trying to balance physical needs against spiritual needs

Aware that the spiritual ones often always seem to lose

New Writing Tablet

New writing tablet
Clean slate to again begin
Those cursive loops
That burrow ever deeper into my memories
Until they hit the magma called truth
And my eyes fill with tears

Coming out...
Acceptance of a deeply interred secret
Am I not the same?
I am not the same
Tomorrows are never mirror images of yesterday

Yet the shifting of my days has begun
Splinters of truth, drunk with a moment's sunlight
Explode into a kaleidoscope of possibilities
Possibilities doomed to fade in the dusk
Until I am ready to share my secret with the world

National Holocaust Remembrance Day

Today is National Holocaust Remembrance Day

In my mind's eye I see the destruction of a civilization

A tsunami of people pulled from every shoreline,
Every country, every city, village, shtetl,
Drowned in the waves of hate and prejudice

A man struggling with his last breath to keep his son afloat,
fearful his strength will give out before the waters recede

A woman praying to the God she cannot see for her young child
to be harbored by someone generous of heart

Barefoot adolescents, dry of tears, fleeing aging parents
and running to safety

I cannot focus on literature and character development
while the roar of millions whispers in my ears pleading to be
remembered

The Sculptor

Earth's compost ready-made for my fingers
Grey, red, gritty or smooth
Each fist-full of slime waiting to be molded
Turning yesterday's memories into tomorrow's treasures

Tenacious textures blend
Yielding as I work
Folding into that oval shape I know so well
Eyes emerging first, to steer pencil point tools
Telling me where to place his nose and lips
As grandfather's face blossoms with a grin
And captures my heart

Love

First Love

Atlantic City voyage with grandmother
Freedom from parental oversight
I'd run to the beach
Through hot sun and scalding sand
The roar of the ocean stirring emotions never shared
I was thirteen

Harry was there
Shirtless and freckled
He was eighteen
Doling beach chairs and cushions for a summer's wage
His smile made my heart dance to a new rhythm
I did not yet understand

Under the beach umbrella, lathered in Coppertone
Far from grandmother's eyes
I'd watch him at work
Fighting for dollar tips
Among ice cream vendors

And like the gulls
That scavenged for crumbs in the vendors wake
My eyes remained glued to Harry
Neither of us seeing in this young girl the woman emerging

I Love You

I love you
    Spoken – face to face
    Whispered – when you sleep
    Dreamed – when I sleep
    Written – on holiday cards, letters, emails
    Heard – across telephone wires
    Penned – in chocolate frosting on birthday cakes
    Celebrated – at marriages, anniversaries
        and new births
    Cried – at death and passings
    Hoped – on long voyages and army deployments

I love you
    What does it mean?
    For this second we are bound together…soul to soul
    A tendril of cosmic energy connects us

I love you
    I see you
    I hear you
    Your imperfections fall like chips of peeling paint
    Revealing the essence of your being
    And I see only the goodness of the universe in your eyes
    Your touch heals and makes me whole

I love you
    You are the light in my life
    And when you say you love me also
    My eyes fill with happy tears

Light

Morning Light
    Shines through my window
        Sun flitting
        Planting butterfly kisses on my closed eyelids
        Sending a kaleidoscope of colors
            cascading across my mind
        Dancing with hopes and dreams
            and magical destinations

Afternoon Light
    Hides behind the wind
    Too busy to be seen
    Growing flowers and children
    Plucking weeds and pushing swings
    Phone calls, doctor visits, endless 'to do's'

But Evening Light
    Is best of all
    Sliding silently under the doorsill
        of my darkened room
    Heralding his footsteps
    I smile in the muted glow of nightfall
    Knowing he has returned safely
    The day's dreams consummated

Prayer

In-Between

It is in the in-between times
    That my mind awakens
        To see the universe most clearly

In-between heartbeats
    Glimpses of light set my soul on fire
        Offering clarity to this world of perpetual chaos

There is a sacred time when the universe reveals herself
    Within the night-clothed shadows
        When the earth feigns sleep

Between the hours of 3 and 5 am
    A universal voice awakens restless spirits from slumber
        And we stare into the darkness
            As if tuning into a conference call from God

And we perceive
    Beyond the sound of our own breath
        In-between our own heartbeats
        That glimpse of golden thread
        That binds us all together
        Into a tightly woven cloth
        And it all makes sense

All in seconds
    Between our heartbeats
        And the birth of each new breath

And then, in darkness
    Warm, comfortable, a smile on our lips
        We drift back to sleep

Only to awaken hours later
    Into this world of daily confusion
        Knowing within our heart there is more
            And we have been seen

Prayer

She stood facing east, toward Jerusalem
Open palms lifted toward the sun
Catching morning rays still fragrant with early dew
Then allowing them to slip between her fingers

Her mantra, a gentle whisper
I ask nothing from the world this day
But to rejoice in its existence
I have nothing to offer but myself

To You who see me most clearly
Please accept this gift of who I am
For it is all that I have